faith. hope. &love

Kai can DO!

for evan. marky. & kai

www.PANDUCORN.com

Meet Kai. He is cute and cuddly. He loves his family, eating fruits, ice cream and cuddling with his mama.

Kai lives in the magical land of rainbows and sunshine.

Kai's mom is a former 80's pop star named
Dreamstar Unicorn. His dad is a tai chi
master and sushi chef name Chi Panda.

This means Kai has both unicorn and panda powers.

His best friends are Kenzo Tiger and Mojo
Monkey. Kenzo is a little more cautious about
new things, while Mojo is more mischievous and
adventurous.

Kai and his friends love playing together and discovering new things.

However, what he loves the most these days is his Mypad, which he recently received as a birthday present. Since then, it has been his best friend and companion.

He never takes his eyes off the tablet.

He walk through fun things, such as birthday parties...

building sand castles at the beach...

and going to the park...

He passed his friends playing in the snow.

His friends say, " Kai Panducorn, come play
with us." But he would reply, "Kai can't do."
All Kai would look at was his Mypad.

13

His mom says "Kai, come help me make cookies." But he would reply to Mama Panducorn, "Kai can't do." He would still keep his eyes glued to his Mypad.

14

Daddy Panducorn say, "Kai ride with me." But he would reply "Kai can't do."

For hours, Kai Panducorn would ignore
everything around him and look only at
his Mypad.

One day, Kai was walking and playing on his Mypad. He was not paying attention and tripped. His Mypad broke upon his fall. He was very sad. 17

But then, he looked up and noticed that a unicorn ice cream party was going on. He had not noticed it before!

He joined in and had so much fun! He
realized all the fun he was missing by playing
only with his Mypad.

Now when Kai's dad asks him to meditate, he says, "Kai can do!"

20

He helps his mom and does chores around the house.

When his friends ask him to ride bikes, Kai says, "Kai can do!"

22

He can now see his family and
friends as the rainbow of his life.

The end

Coming Soon!
Kai Panducorn and his Magical Bobo
Color with Kai!
Panda & Unicorn Coloring Book

WWW.PANDUCORN.com

About the Authors

Kathy V. Tran & Aiki Tran currently live in Houston, Texas with their 3 boys, Labrador retriever, and tortoises. Their sons are the inspiration for their stories and the motivator to keep improving. Kathy's goal is to find the best ice cream in the world. Aiki is motivated to create a roadmap for the boys to experience life to the fullest.

Core Values of Panducorn

i am unique
i am loving
i am valuable

i am connected
i am compassionate
i am capable

i am adaptable
i am creative
i am magical!

Key Values
- Kai can do, so can you!
- Friends and family priorities
- Experiencing life

Questions for Kai's friends
- How many rainbows do you see on each page?
- What can you do to help mom and dad?
- Who is hidding in all the pages?

www.panducorn.com